ANGELS
IN ART

ANGELS
IN ART

BELINDA WILKINSON

Picture selection by
Julia Brown

STUDIO EDITIONS
LONDON

Frontispiece: Simone Martini (1284-1344),
The Annunciation *(detail).*

This edition published 1994 by
Studio Editions Ltd
Princess House, 50 Eastcastle Street
London, W1N 7AP, England

Design by Michael R Carter
Printed and bound in the Slovak Republic

ISBN 1 85891 170 2

INTRODUCTION

Angels are the winged and radiant messengers of God, who fly between heaven and earth, mediating between God and man. In the *Purgatorio*, Dante describes them as the bright birds of God, indicating their heavenly role and nature. In art, too, angels appear with the wings of a bird, but with the figure of a perfect man. Although common to Christianity, Islam and Judaism, angels are most fully expressed in the art of the Christian west.

Angels first appear in fourth-century Byzantine art. Wholly Greek in origin, they recall the flying deities of the Classical world. By the fifth century, radiant *nimbi* (haloes) surround angels' heads, creating an archetypal image which has survived to the present day. At this early stage, other quite different angels emerge — the flaming, six-winged seraphim and revolving ophanim — both inspired by scripture, such as the Books of Isaiah and Ezekiel. These exotic creatures belong to the highest orders or 'choirs' of angels, but although they were popular in Byzantium, they featured less often as art styles grew more naturalistic.

The full heavenly host was codified in a fifth-century work, *De Hierarchia Celesti*, based on the visions of the prophets, and ascribed to Dionysius the Areopagite. In his classic work, he describes nine choirs of angels in three hierarchies: seraphim, cherubim and ophanim, who surround God in perpetual adoration; dominions, virtues and powers, who govern the stars and elements; princedoms, archangels and angels, who protect nations and guide the souls of men. *De Hierarchia Celesti* did much to shape early symbolism, although complete angelic hierarchies rarely appear, except in early Byzantine churches, such as Ivirôn on Mount Athos in Greece. On the whole, western artists focused on the angels closest to earth, although the highest orders did receive some attention.

Common to all angels are the symbolic attributes of light, flight and heavenly beauty. Their beauty is, inevitably, expressed in human terms and in contemporary styles of art. Angelic faces are typically radiant, youthful and serene, while graceful figures are clad in robes that are often Classical, though sometimes priestly and fashionable. Early Byzantine angels are still and gracious with the grave eyes and serious air of their Greek models. By the Middle Ages they have become ethereal and immaterial, often disappearing in a whirl of robes or melting into cloud. Fluid and expressive, Gothic angels sometimes share in the human drama, as do Giotto's distracted spirits (*see* Plate 3). Those of the Renaissance, such as Melozzo's Gabriel or Botticelli's choirs, reach a

Tapestry in wool and linen, Upper Egypt (5th century).
A winged victory or early angel, based on the flying Nike
of ancient Greece, bears a jewelled cross symbolizing the
Christian faith.

peak of sublime grace perhaps never seen again.
During the Baroque era, many angels emerge as
fresh and candid infants or cherubs (*see* Plate 16),
based on the Classical gods, Eros and Cupid.
Adult Baroque angels, by contrast, are depicted as
splendid soaring beings, robed in swirling draper-
ies. The dreamy Italianate creations of the Pre-
Raphaelites and late Romantics revive some
aspects of the Renaissance, while many modern
angels recall the simplicity and spirituality of the
earliest portrayals (*see* Plates 24 & 25).

Life-giving light is a universal symbol of divinity, reflected in the angels' luminous forms. Early

Mosaic (early 6th century), The Separation of the Goats from the Sheep. *The earliest angels emerge fully winged and radiant, with the gracious air of their Greek models.*

Biblical descriptions, as in the Book of Ezekiel, emphasize their brilliance as being 'like burning coals of fire'. Artists express this heavenly radiance in a variety of ways. Angelic faces glow; angelic robes are luminous, sometimes richly coloured or embroidered to create a jewelled effect. The clearest symbols of divine light, however, are the angel's nimbus and flame of holy fire. The Latin *nimbus*, meaning both aura and rain-cloud, perhaps recalls the myth that angels are born from raindrops shaken from the Lord's

Guido Reni (1575—1642), The Abduction of Helen *(detail).*
Cupid, the Roman god of love, served as a model for Baroque
winged cherubs, whether mythological or religious.

wings. The earliest nimbi were based on the star-like blue haloes of Classical sky and sun gods. Angelic nimbi may be coloured, transparent, gilded, plain or striated to create a sparkling effect. Although nimbi seem to disappear after the Renaissance, they re-emerge in various styles in Pre-Raphaelite and modern art. The angelic flame, symbolizing the light of divine intelligence, appears in a stylized form in Byzantine art, but more often as a decorative jewel in Renaissance and Romantic paintings.

Angels also show their divine nature in serenity and composure (*see* Plate 5). Some angels, however, reflect human sorrow and care, especially in scenes of Christ's deposition or the trials of the saints; and the archangel Michael expresses unusual sternness in scenes of battle or the Last Judgement (*see* Plate 17).

Wings symbolize flight, the freedom of the skies and the power to bridge the gulf between God and man, heaven and earth. The great folded wings of Byzantium are majestic and stylized, sometimes no more than a snowy outline (*see* Plate 1), sometimes decorated with swirling patterns. Medieval wings are lighter, more fanciful, often finely fluted and brightly coloured in many tiers. Star-like cherubim and seraphim appear with tiny heads submerged in one, two or three pairs of wings. The seraph's ruby wings represent fiery love, while the cherub's blue wings suggest divine wisdom. Renaissance and Baroque artists modelled their wings closely on the most beautiful and splendid of birds, such as swans and peacocks. Peacocks also symbolize eternity and the countless eyes of the seraphim. Renaissance angels glide effortlessly through the air, while those of the Baroque era soar and dive in dramatic displays of flight (*see* Plate 15).

Opposite: Lorenzo Monaco (c. 1372–1422), The Coronation of the Virgin (detail). A minstrel angel plays a portative organ, a small, portable instrument, particularly popular in concerts of angels.

Angels appear in most scenes of the Christian drama, from the Creation through to the Apocalypse. Music accompanies their every work, and their concerts glorify God, Christ, the Virgin and saints. As the guardians of mankind, angels accompany people on their journey through life, inspiring, consoling, protecting and punishing. Finally, with a trumpet call, they awaken the souls of the dead, steer them gently through the trials of Judgement, and lead them, dancing, through the Gates of Paradise.

Pietro Perugino (c. 1445–1523), The Vallombrosa Altarpiece *(detail). This is possibly a seraph, one of the highest choirs of angels. According to the Book of Isaiah, "each one had six wings; with twain he covered his face, and with twain he covered his feet, and with twain he did fly."*

THE —
PLATES

PLATE 1
San Pablo de Casseres, Spain (13th century)
The Last Judgement
DETAIL

In scenes of the Last Judgement, angels are often depicted blowing their trumpets to raise the souls of the dead, as in this striking tomb mural from the Romanesque church of San Pablo in Spain. Medieval wall-painters had to tell their story in clear and simple terms, with flowing lines and bold designs that would impress from afar. Here, the angels' wide white haloes, fresh open faces, large burning eyes and great stylized wings are all presented in their most graphic and essential form. Although the range of colour pigment was restricted in the remote valleys, creative artists produced a subtle mix of tones. The angels' faces are delicately modelled in flesh tints, probably achieved by mixing lime white with cinnabar and ochre. Precious blue, rarely used in Southern churches, is also absent here, yet a striking effect is achieved by setting the luminous figures against a warm, earthy background. The angels' stark Byzantine wings contrast with their gracious stance and tranquil air which look forward to the Gothic style.

PLATE 2

The Ingeborg Psalter (1213)
Abraham and the Angels

While Abraham sat in his tent door in 'the heat of the day', he was visited by three men who foretold the birth of his son, Isaac. The story, from the Book of Genesis, is told here in two parts: in the upper tier, Abraham greets his heavenly visitors while his wife, Sarah, peeps out from their 'tent', suggested by a decorative canopy. The three 'men' are all fully winged and radiant, reflecting the fact that Abraham regarded them as heavenly. All three carry sceptres, the first tipped with a fleur-de-lys, one of Gabriel's attributes. They walk on rippling desert sand, suggested by a vibrant onyx-like pattern. In the lower tier, Abraham offers the angels a calf, 'tender and good', while Sarah brings in the three cakes he has instructed her to make.

The Ingeborg Psalter, named after Queen Ingeborg of Denmark, blends many traditions. The two-tier design and formal gestures are Byzantine in origin, while the austere linework and burnished splendour reflect the English manuscript tradition. The glowing colours, possibly inspired by Gothic stained glass, and the decorative borders look forward to the French style.

Si come il leur dona a mamgier.

PLATE 3
Giotto (*c.* 1267−1337)
The Lamentation

Giotto's tiny spirits, immersed in cloud, express an unexpected intensity of grief. Such humanly distraught and expressive angels are unusual in Christian art. Sorrowful gods do grieve for 'mortal men' in ancient Greek art, but they express their feelings in a restrained manner, much like Giotto's frozen people below. Giotto's despairing angels perhaps reflect his dramatic temper; they also perhaps express the idea that only the great angels share in divine foreknowledge, while the smaller angels, like these distracted spirits, remain unaware of Christ's destiny.

The group around Christ complement the angels' grief in a numb and stoic way. The whole scene is Classically restrained, ordered and bare. Yet the grave mood is lifted by touches of Gothic grace: the Virgin cradles Christ's head in a tender way, recalling her earlier role in Giotto's *Nativity*. The Magdalen, supporting Christ's feet, also reflects a happier episode when she washed His feet. Although the bare tree and rocky ridge echo the stark and wintry mood, the tree also symbolizes eventual rebirth.

PLATE 4

Guariento de Arpo (*fl.* 1338–70)
Archangel Michael

One of Michael's chief duties in medieval art was to 'weigh the souls of the dead' at the Last Judgement to measure each person's just deserts. Known as psychostasis, this was an ancient duty inherited from the Classical spirit guides or psychopomps, Mercury and Hermes, and the Egyptian Anubis. Michael balances a pair of golden scales, in either pan of which a small soul kneels in prayer. Risen souls were often depicted as tiny naked people, recalling Classical images of infant souls. Usually, the heavier soul was meant to be the more virtuous, though painters differed on this point and the heavier one in this case seems to be the least virtuous. He is under attack from the side by a furtive black demon who tries to tip the scales.

Arpo's rather gentle and gracious Michael is robed in white and gold, symbolizing his purity. The colour of his flame-red wings suggests divine love. His decorative gold corselet is a delicate reflection of the armour usually worn by this angelic warrior. Arpo was a disciple of Giotto whose influence can be seen in the angel's sculptural figure and finely modelled face.

PLATE 5

French School (*c.* 1395)
The Wilton Diptych

DETAIL

This heavenly vision in blue is part of a diptych commemorating the coronation of Richard II in 1377. The boy king appears on the left-hand panel, kneeling in prayer and surrounded by his patron saints who commend him to the Virgin and infant Christ. On the right-hand panel, the Virgin stands in a heavenly meadow surrounded by eleven radiant angels, all wearing the king's livery: the white hart and gold antlers. As the infant Christ leans forward to bless the youthful king, His halo shimmers with the motifs of His passion: three nails and a crown of thorns.

The whole scene is infused with Gothic grace and fancy. A lyrical rhythm flows through the line of paired wings and radiant rosy faces. Dainty motifs abound, painted with exquisite care in the French miniaturist style. The Parisian Court style is apparent, too, in the courteous and reticent characters who show their tender feelings in delicate hand gestures and sensitive expressions.

PLATE 6

The Wonders of Creation and the Rarities of Things (15th century)
Jabrā'īl

Jabrā'īl, an Islamic archangel, is generally thought to be the Angel of Revelation who inspired the Prophet Muhammad to write the sacred Koran, and escorted him on his night journey to heaven. This gentle guardian is usually depicted as a delicate youth, as in this exquisite Persian miniature. Jabrā'īl's perfection and grace are expressed in delicate colours and flowing lines, in his swirling plaits, and in his light, joyful step as he strides across the heavens blowing his annunciation trumpet. The clouds are suggested by fluffy scrolls, recalling cloud bands from early Mongolian manuscripts.

The Wonders of Creation by Al-Qazvini was first produced in the fifteenth century, based on a Persian manuscript of the same title compiled in the fourteenth century. Al-Qazvini's popular manuscript ran to many editions, sometimes illustrated with over 400 jewel-like miniatures. This edition reflects the art of the Mamluk period from *c*. 1250 to 1500: Jabrā'īl is typically expressive, fluid and archetypal; he emerges from a golden sky, suggesting the light of Islam's many heavens.

وَمِنهُم جَبرَئِيل

فَإِذا بَيْنَهُ اَمِينُ الْوَحِي وَخازِنُ الْقُدُسِ وَيُقالُ لَهُ اِنَّهُ الرُّوحُ الْاَمِينُ وَالرُّوحُ الْقُدُسِ
وَالنّامُوسُ الْاَكْبَرُ وَطاوُسُ الْمَلائِكَةِ جاءَتْ فِي الْقُرْآنِ اَنَّ اللّٰهَ خَفّالَهُ اِذا بَعَثَكُمْ بِالْوَحْي
سَمِعَ اَهْلُ السَّمآءِ صَلْصَلَةٌ كَجَرِّ السَّلْسَلَةِ عَلَى الصَّفا فَيُصْعَقُونَ وَكانَ الّذِينَ كَذَلِكَ
حَتَّى يَأْتِيَهُمْ جَبرَئِيل فَإِذا جاءَ هُمْ فَزَعَ عَنْ قُلُوبِهِمْ فَقالُوا يا جَبرَئِيل ما ذا قالَ رَبُّكَ
فَيَقُولُ الْحَقَّ فَيُنادُونَ الْحَقَّ الْحَقَّ وَجاءَتِ الْجِنانُ النَّبِيِّ صَلّى اللّٰهُ عَلَيهِ وَآلِهِ وَسَلَّمَ
فَقالَ لِجَبرَئِيل اِنِّي اَحبَّ اَنْ اَراكَ عَلَى صُورَتِكَ فَقالَ اِنَّكَ لا تُطِيقُ ذَلِكَ

PLATE 7

Studio of Fra Angelico (*c.* 1420–30)
The Last Judgement

In many traditions Paradise is depicted as an enclosed garden, garden island or green isle, sealed off in time and space. The word itself derives from Greek and Persian terms for park or walled garden. In Gothic art, paradise gardens became particularly popular, reflecting perhaps the mystical trend for expressing spiritual ideas in naturalistic form: the flowers are depicted with rapture, but also with close attention to detail.

In this shimmering vision of paradise, a throng of angels leads the blessed towards the City of God. The angels' ring dance or *ballo dei angeli* alludes to the dance of choirs around the throne of God. Angelico was possibly inspired by some lines from a poem by the Franciscan monk, Jacopone da Todi: 'Dance they all in a heavenly circle, Blessed ones in Christ's own garden...'

Angelico's colours are pure, transparent and heraldic, painted with a filigree delicacy and decorated with gold to sparkling effect. For such sublime work, as much as for his gentle character, the artist earned his reverential title.

PLATE 8

Hans Memlinc (*c.* 1430/40−94)
Angels Making Music

Music accompanies angels' every work. Concerts are played around God, Christ, and the Virgin, expressing perpetual adoration, while minstrel angels inspire and console both the Saints and humanity. Memlinc's three minstrels form part of a heavenly choir of ten appearing on a great triptych painted for the church of Najera in Spain. Like many Renaissance angels, they play contemporary instruments: the angel on the left plucks a psaltery, an ancient zither-like instrument; the middle musician plays a *tromba marina*, which sounds like a trumpet; while the far one plucks a lute.

Memlinc was an original colourist. His luminous golds, emeralds, violets and blues were applied with miniaturist care to create a richly glowing effect. The spiritual, starlit atmosphere is produced by subtle lighting: dawn light shines through the clouds, casting gold and emerald hues across the angels' silky robes and peacock wings. Memlinc's remote and dreamy characters perhaps lack the emotional power of other northern painters, yet radiate an arresting grace and candour.

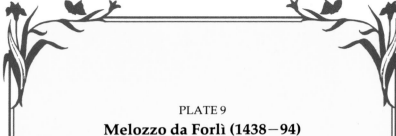

PLATE 9
Melozzo da Forlì (1438 – 94)
Angel of the Annunciation

This is one of a pair of panels which may have served originally as organ shutters. On the right-hand panel, the Virgin stands in quiet contemplation, hands folded serenely on her breast; while here, Gabriel, a model of Classical beauty, alights with swift step and flowing robes. His uplifted wings and flying sash evoke a sense of urgent flight, indicating the importance of his mission. With one upraised hand, he blesses the Virgin; with the other, he holds a white lily, symbol of purity. Gabriel's white rippling robes are painted in fluid, crystal lines, recalling Mantegna's wiry style. Gabriel's face is typically delicate, but also alert and sensitive, gazing with a quizzical glance at the silent Virgin. In the distance, a dark mountain melts into the luminous sky, adding to the stillness of the moment which lifts the whole scene out of time.

PLATE 10

Carlo Crivelli (*fl*. 1457−93)

The Annunciation, with Saint Emidius

DETAIL

O n the Feast of the Annunciation in 1482, the papal town of Ascoli Piceno in Italy was granted limited rights of self-government. To commemorate the event, the people of Ascoli commissioned Crivelli to paint this unusual and elaborate annunciation which combines political and religious themes. Crivelli has set the annunciation in a street of the ideal town, a model of which can be seen in the hands of the town's patron saint, Emidius, who kneels beside Gabriel.

Every inch of the complex scene is adorned with pattern and colour. Marble and masonry, silk and brocade are described with precision in Crivelli's intricate wiry style. A rich priestly atmosphere pervades the scene, enhanced by the jewelled vestments. Crivelli's curious stylized characters are compelling if rather remote, their robes sumptuous yet cold. The gourd and apple at the edge of the picture reflect Crivelli's love of inner meanings. The apple symbolizes the New Adam (Christ), while the gourd represents redemption.

PLATE 11

Sandro Botticelli (1445–1510)
Mystic Nativity

Botticelli's spirited nativity represents not just the birth of Christ but also His future reign of peace. The angels carry olive, the emblem of peace, and they twirl heavenly crowns and banderoles inscribed with joyful messages. In the foreground, three affectionate angels embrace men in goodwill, while stricken demons scurry into holes. The joyful choir in the sky dances in a circle, a motif possibly inspired by Dante's *Paradiso*, in which he describes the nine choirs of angels surrounding God in nine concentric circles. The angels' rippling robes recall those of the dancing Greek Maenades (devotees of Dionysus), depicted on Hellenistic relief. In the midst of all this swirling activity, the devoted Virgin, symbolically larger than the rest, kneels in quiet adoration before Christ while from either side, angels guide the kings and shepherds to worship.

The whole scene is joyful and vital, painted in Botticelli's fluid linear style. Only the rigid stable seems at odds with the flowing design, yet this apparent discord is relieved by the line of angels and dawn clouds in the golden sky above.

PLATE 12

Follower of Andrea del Verrocchio
(*c.* 1470 – 75)
Tobias and the Angel

Tobias' eventful journey was a popular theme in Florentine art, and the subject was often commissioned to commemorate a son's long journey. The story, from the Book of Tobit, tells of Tobias' trip to a distant city to collect a debt for his blind father, Tobit. The boy was accompanied on his journey by the archangel Raphael incognito. At the river Tigris, Tobias was attacked by a 'great fish', but under Raphael's guidance, he caught and gutted the fish, setting aside the heart, liver and gall for use in healing.

In this scene, both travellers wear wayfarers' robes of the latest fashion; rich gold thread shimmers on their sleeves and sashes. They stride with an easy grace and serene air, reminiscent of Verrocchio's polished style. The left hands of both figures are identical, suggesting a common model. On the fish's belly, a fine crimson line marks the point of incision, while the small metal box held by Raphael possibly contains the healing parts. The rolling landscape is exquisitely described, though some of the rocks are now fading as is Tobias' companionable dog.

PLATE 13
Leonardo da Vinci (1452−1519)
Annunciation

DETAIL

Known as the Uffizi *Annunciation* this is now generally thought to have been designed by Leonardo and painted by him at least in part. Certain features are characteristic of his early style, such as Gabriel's carefully detailed wings and the melting landscape in the distance. Although the wings have been heavily over-painted and lengthened, Leonardo modelled them on a bird's and they apparently fitted the angel's shoulders with ease. Gabriel's sleeve, for which a sketch by Leonardo exists, again reflects the master's close observation of nature.

The annunciation is set traditionally outside a loggia within a walled garden, the *hortus conclusus*, symbolic of the Virgin's chastity and fruitfulness. But Leonardo's lovely garden is not simply sym-bolic: his flowers seem to ripple with a natural vitality. Similarly, his moody landscape, the dark trees, misty sea and luminous sky all evoke a dusky brooding atmosphere.

PLATE 14

Suceviţa Monastery, Romania
(16th century)
The Ladder of Virtue

DETAIL

A ladder, rope or rainbow bridge linking heaven and earth is a universal symbol of ascension. In this radiant blue fresco, the souls of the virtuous climb a moral ladder leading to heaven. At the top, God reaches out a helping hand, while the serried ranks of angels advance with victorious crowns and scarves with which to adorn the Blessed. In Byzantine and Gothic art, such scarves or napkins are sometimes used to carry souls from earth to heaven, recalling images of the Classical gods, Iris and Mercury, bearing souls wrapped in narrow bands of cloth. While some souls cling valiantly to the Ladder of Virtue, others topple with flailing limbs into the eager arms of small black demons.

The celestial blue sky, painted on a green base, sparkles with white stars. The angels' serene faces, their fluted gold-tipped wings and gilded haloes, and the brilliant blue throughout reveal a strong Byzantine influence. Yet the acrobatic souls are unusually expressive and mobile, reflecting the humorous qualities of Moldavian folk art.

PLATE 15
Adam Elsheimer (1578–1610)
The Stoning of St Stephen

DETAIL

Elsheimer's great angel dives headfirst to earth in a fearless godlike flight. He carries the martyr's palm to Stephen, who falls beneath the stones of an angry crowd. The story, from the Acts of the Apostles, tells how Stephen had upset the Sanhedrin (supreme Jewish council) with an outspoken sermon, at the end of which he gazed up to heaven and saw a vision which further incited the crowd: ' "Behold, I see the heavens opened, and the Son of man standing on the right hand of God." Then they cried out...and ran upon him with one accord.'

Elsheimer has captured something of Stephen's electrifying vision. The heavens radiate a thundery supernatural glow and pour forth luminous whirling angels; the mingled lights of heaven and earth create a stormy mystical mood. Elsheimer's gift for depicting the play of light earned him the title 'painter-poet', and possibly inspired Claude, Rubens and Rembrandt. Although he has painted his vision with great delicacy, the broad design remains clear and dramatic, the figures powerful and statuesque.

PLATE 16

Philippe de Champaigne (1602−74)
The Adoration of the Shepherds

DETAIL

Baroque angels often appear as tiny winged infants or cherubs, not unlike Cupid's playful companions. Known loosely as *putti*, from the Latin *putus* meaning 'little man', they derive ultimately from the Greek Erotes, winged spirits who accompanied a man's soul on his journey through life. Champaigne's three golden cherubs have accompanied the shepherds on their journey to Bethlehem to see the newborn Christ. The Infant's radiant glow casts golden shafts across the cherubs hovering in the night sky − an effect possibly inspired by Correggio. Their translucent blue and mauve robes symbolize divine wisdom. Twirling in the breeze, the cherubs' golden banderole carries a message of hope and joy, as related in St Luke's Gospel, 'Glory be to God in the highest and on earth peace and goodwill to men.' The glowing night sky reflects Champaigne's early talent for landscape, while his flair for character portrayal is clearly revealed in the candid gaze of the wide-eyed cherubs.

PLATE 17

Unknown Artist (18th century)
Archangel Michael

Michael's dynamic and unflinching character is clearly expressed in this powerful
Greek icon. The archangel's unsheathed
sword and iron corselet denote his sombre duties
as Captain of the Heavenly Host and Lord of
Souls, while his flaming robes and tongue of fire
symbolize fiery love. Michael's finely modelled
Byzantine face is illuminated with a rosy light from
the left and slightly from above which creates a
flickering candlelit effect, enhancing the intensity
of the portrait.

Icons are sacred objects of devotion, expressions
of living divinity. Painted by consecrated monks,
they are designed to evoke a sense of wonder,
mystery and awe. Precious jewels, burnished gold
and flickering church light all contribute to this
aim, but it is usually the eyes, especially in frontal
icons, which hold the viewer spellbound.
Michael's stern expression is not without under-
standing, and as he gazes intently, we gain the
impression of a living spiritual presence.

PLATE 18

William Blake (1757—1827)
Christ in the Sepulchre
Guarded by Angels

Blake was a visionary artist, poet and mystic who rebelled against mainstream art, seeking to express his powerful visions in an original way. In doing so, he evolved a rich mythical imagery and a distinctive linear style, clear, fluid and vigorous. Blake's fertile imagination absorbed and developed ideas from many sources but he was especially fond of Gothic art, as can be seen in these striking figures, possibly modelled on tombstones in Westminster Abbey.

The strength of the design lies in its simplicity and order. The formal balance could seem static and contrived, yet the angels' luminous forms glow in mid-air. A sense of serenity pervades the scene, created in part by the theme, by the still, sleeping Christ, but also by the deliberate order and timeless mood. Yet, although the angels seem suspended in space and time, their subtly flowing forms create a quietly expectant atmosphere. The whole arresting design recalls some words from Blake's *Vala* or *The Four Zoas*: 'hovering high over his head, Two winged immortal shapes...Their wings joined at the zenith overhead.'

PLATE 19

Edward Burne-Jones (1833−98)
Angeli Laudantes

The Pre-Raphaelite painter, Edward Burne-Jones, produced many tapestry and stained-glass designs for the firm of Morris & Co. This glowing tapestry reflects the firm's distinctive style, richly intricate, but crisp and clear in concept. Woven in wools and silks, it was produced on a cotton warp at the Merton Abbey works in 1894.

The minstrels are based on a cartoon designed for a window in Salisbury Cathedral. Burne-Jones' graceful Italianate figures and sculptural robes reflect his passion for Renaissance art, yet a curious fairy-like quality pervades the work, perhaps created by the angels' fey and distant air, by their unusual lyres and flowery background. The angels' gossamer haloes and holy white flames contrast curiously with their plush crimson wings and sumptuous robes to create a rich but otherworldly effect. William Morris and Henry Dearle (director of the Merton Abbey works) designed the floral border and *millefleurs* garden which rises up all around like an enchanted forest in a fairytale.

PLATE 20

William Morris (1834–96)
Minstrel Angel

This jewelled angel is one of five appearing in the east window of St Michael's, Tilehurst, near Reading. Designed by William Morris, it was produced by Morris & Co in 1869. Morris' unique talents as a colourist and designer, and his passion for medieval imagery inspired the firm's bright enamelled style, apparent in this richly coloured glass. A glowing medieval atmosphere is created, not only by the mosaic of pure colour, but also by subtle decorative details, such as the angel's medieval rebec, a stringed instrument played in the open air during village fairs. To create the flesh tints on the angel's quiet contemplative face, Morris applied thin washes of reddish enamel, delicately staining the white glass. He decorated the angel's shimmering alb with one of his gold-leaf motifs, and his love of nature's flowing patterns is seen in the deep blue cloud whirls and flaming yellow stars which sparkle in the midnight sky.

PLATE 21

Paul Gauguin (1848—1903)
Jacob Wrestling with the Angel

The mysterious conflict between Jacob and the angel has been variously expressed in art as man's battle with himself, with God or with the Devil. In this modern interpretation, Gauguin stresses the spiritual intensity of the struggle, setting the event in the mind's eye of the Breton women who experience a communal vision inspired by a Sunday sermon. The tiny wrestlers struggle alone on a glowing red field, separated literally and metaphorically from the natural world of the women. The diagonal tree and sharp shift in perspective and colour highlight the division between the inner world of experience and the outer world of appearance. Gauguin's focus on the inner life was pioneering at the time, and in his efforts to convey an intense visionary experience, he has blended many styles. The flaming colours recall Gothic stained glass; the bold outline, medieval woodblock; while the close grappling combat of the wrestlers and the diagonal tree reflect Japanese woodblock design.

PLATE 22
John Duncan (1866−1945)
St Bride

The Celtic revivalist, John Duncan, merges Celtic and Christian symbolism in this sparkling fantasy. St Bride was a fifth-century Irish saint, who founded an order of nuns in Kildare. Legend tells of her miraculous journey from the Scottish island of Iona to Bethlehem on the night of Christ's birth. Duncan illustrates this story in his bright, ethereal style. The angels carry the sleeping saint across Iona's foamy sea. The childlike figure and her white night-robe symbolize the saint's purity and trance-like state. Duncan's jewelled angels wear copes embroidered with the story of Christ's life. The startling spiritual atmosphere is enhanced by the angels' soaring flight beyond the picture frame.

The fresh blue seascape recalls the idyllic shores of Iona, a Druid retreat, famed for its crystal-clear light, and much frequented by Duncan and his Celtic friends.

PLATE 23

Frank Cadogan Cowper (1877−1958)
Francis of Assisi and the Heavenly Messenger

DETAIL

Cowper's painting is devotional in theme, depicting St Francis at prayer, consoled by an angel. In this detail, the minstrel angel plays a heavenly tune to the saint who listens in rapture below, his Bible discarded at his feet.

This unusual angel, perched on a tree like a bird, seems as natural as the doves at St Francis' feet. The effect is achieved by the earthy pastoral setting, and by the birdlike quality, colour and texture of the angel's rainbow-coloured wings. Another extraordinary feature is the luminous halo, defined so sharply that it should appear unreal, yet, by reflecting the brilliant sunlight, seeming completely natural.

Cowper developed a talent for describing the texture and colour of fabric, and a passion for historical detail, seen here in the angel's priestly vestments and Renaissance viol. The gnarled tree trunk, pearly sky and sunlit field complete the summery scene.

PLATE 24
Marc Chagall (1887–1985)
Flying Angel

Chagall began designing stained glass in the 1950s, inspired by the jewelled windows of Chartres Cathedral, and he found it the perfect medium for his brilliant colour and mythical vision. This window on the north side of All Saints, Tudely, Kent, is one of five designed by Chagall, and executed by Charles Marq of Reims, a glassmaker with whom he enjoyed a long collaboration. It depicts a flying angel, a recurrent motif in Chagall's dreamlike imagery. Chagall's angels are sometimes light and buoyant, sometimes dark and haunting, but always luminous in pure colour, and compelling in graphic line. The angel in this tranquil blue window emerges out of the sky, shimmering in the brilliant light, just pausing to gaze with a gentle, quizzical air on the world below.

The rest of the glass in the church is also by Chagall, the earliest being in the east window, a moving memorial to Sarah d'Avigdor-Godsmid, a girl who was drowned at sea. In the south window, yellow abstract designs reflect the warm light of the sun, while on the north side, quiet blues and mauves spread a calm, contemplative light.

PLATE 25

Michael Chase (*b*. 1915)
Angel over Le Besset

A ngels often feature in the paintings of Michael Chase who comments on this aspect of his work: 'I am not aware of having deliberately set out to paint pictures with angels in them; nonetheless, I have always been drawn by their visual qualities...' The angels of the Italian masters, of Botticelli and El Greco have especially inspired his work.

In this scene, an angel passes over the rooftops of Le Besset, a small hamlet set in the hill country of the Cévennes in France. A sparkling atmosphere pervades the tranquil landscape, which is painted in translucent watercolours and crisp, fluid lines. Chase's simple but striking forms reflect his approach and technique, of which he says: 'I am not a recorder of scenes in the sense that I do not sit down in front of a subject and seek to represent it in a painting as a photographer might do in a photograph. On the other hand, the 'thing seen' does establish for me a visual starting point; indeed, I fill countless sketchbooks with drawings carried out on the spot, but the actual painting takes place in the studio, and the result I think of as an evocation.'

PICTURE ACKNOWLEDGEMENTS

The author and publishers would like to thank the following artists, collectors, galleries and photographic libraries for permission to reproduce their illustrations:

INTRODUCTION
Frontispiece: Uffizi, Florence (Scala, Florence)
Courtesy of the Board of Trustees of the Victoria & Albert Museum, London
(Bridgeman Art Library, London)
S. Apollinare Nuovo, Ravenna (Scala)
Musée du Louvre, Paris (Bridgeman Art Library)
The National Gallery, London
Galleria dell' Accademia, Florence (Bridgeman Art Library)

PLATES
 1 Museo Diocesano de Solsona, Lerida (Index/Bridgeman Art Library)
 2 Musée Condé, Chantilly (Giraudon/Bridgeman Art Library)
 3 Scrovegni Chapel, Padua (E. T. Archive, London)
 4 & Cover (detail) Museo Bottacin e Museo Civico, Padua (Bridgeman Art Library)
 5 The National Gallery, London
 6 The British Museum, London
 7 Museo di San Marco dell' Angelico, Florence (Bridgeman Art Library)
 8 Koninklijk Museum voor Schone Kunsten, Antwerp (Bridgeman Art Library)
 9 Uffizi, Florence (Bridgeman Art Library)
10 The National Gallery, London
11 The National Gallery, London
12 The National Gallery, London
13 Uffizi, Florence (Scala)
14 Sucevita Monastery, Rumania (E. T. Archive)
15 The National Gallery of Scotland, Edinburgh (Bridgeman Art Library)
16 By permission of the Trustees of the Wallace Collection, London (Bridgeman Art Library)
17 Private Collection (Bridgeman Art Library)
18 Courtesy of the Board of Trustees of the Victoria & Albert Museum, London
    (Bridgeman Art Library)
19 Courtesy of the Board of Trustees of the Victoria & Albert Museum, London
    (Bridgeman Art Library)
20 Photo. Ann S Dean, Malvern (Bridgeman Art Library)
21 The National Gallery of Scotland, Edinburgh
22 The National Gallery of Scotland, Edinburgh
23 Christie's, London (Bridgeman Art Library) © The Artist
24 All Saints, Tudeley, Kent (Bridgeman Art Library)
25 Private Collection (Bridgeman Art Library) © The Artist